DISCOVERING *You*

NICKY YARBOROUGH

faith books&MORE

Suwanee, Georgia

Scripture quotations taken from the Amplified Bible
First published by Faith Books & MORE
ISBN 978-0-9845779-4-1

Printed in the United States of America.

This book is printed on acid-free paper.

fai h books&MORE

3255 Lawrenceville-Suwanee Rd.
Suite P250
Suwanee, GA 30024
publishing@faithbooksandmore.com
www.faithbooksandmore.com

Layout and design by
www.kenwarddesigns.com

Dedication

I dedicate this book to my daughter, Keri
and my son, Ron.
I Love You.

Acknowledgements

First, I would like to thank my Lord and Saviour, Jesus Christ. I would also like to thank L.Michelle Hayes (L.Michelle Media), my assistant, for all the hard-work and support throughout the years. Special thanks to my mom (Bertha Howard) for being there no matter what.

And Special thanks also to you, the reader, who today will realize

God wants better for your Life, and by Faith, you shall receive it.

Contents

Foreword

For years, my bathroom mirror was the closest I could get to discovering the real me. When I was child…I understood my identity to mean…Brown hair, brown eyes, brown skin…and a slender face. Combine those images…with the social mirrors of friend, family, and world views of me…by the time I became an adult, I had let those things determine who I was and who I could be. Then came 2004…when I was laid off from my dream job…and the identity I had worked so hard to build…was in a moment…stripped away. I realized then…that I wasn't calling the shots in my Life…and that getting beyond this…would mean getting beyond "Me."

That year, I met Nicky Yarborough, and in my distress and search for answers, she…in a few words brought wisdom and calm. Simply spoken, she said…*"You Have To Let Go Of The Rope!"* Over the years, that has come to mean different things for me…but at that period of uncertainty…it meant one thing. I was going to have to release the Life and Identity that I had come up with on my own… and submit to something greater.

'Discovering You' is the purest form of the wisdom that God gave Nicky to share with me that day. This book is a step-by-step guide to help you through the process of moving forward with Purpose…even when Life goes completely off plan. Written in everyday language, Nicky's Life examples and realistic ministry approach will connect with your heart. You will not only understand the new you…you will be equipped to live out your true destiny.

Looking back on it now, 2004 was the best year of my Life. It was the year I finally stopped existing and began to Live. Now is your opportunity to do the same. As Nicky would say, *"Let Go Of The Rope!"* I am a Living Witness that it's the best free-fall you'll ever take!!!

Let Go and Live!!!! I'm Excited For You!!!
Keisha "L.Michelle" Hayes

Introduction

WHY AM I HERE?

It's one of the most widely asked questions in the world…one that many of us have pondered at some time or another. Why Am I Here? We know the answer defies human comprehension. Still, throughout Life we ask it anyway, hoping to get to the bottom of our current existence before it's too late. 'Why Me, and Why Now," you ask? The answer to this great mystery is found on the inside of you.

Today, as you read this book, God will reveal more about the "Real You" that lives on the inside. The more that is revealed…the more your question of "Why You Are Here" will be answered. As you move forward, your assignment is simple. Read with great expectation and even greater determination to "Discover You" and Live the Life God has intended. Now Is Your Time!

I.

Purpose

We are assured and know that (God being a partner in their labor) all things work together and are (fitting into a plan) for good to and for those who love God and are called according to (His) design and purpose.
Romans 8:28 AMP

The Big Question???

I have always had a lot of questions. Especially back in my childhood days…as a young girl growing up in Quincy, FL. I was one of five in Ma's (my mom) single-wide trailer…where plenty of love seemed to overshadow the finer things of life that we didn't have at the time. I can remember walking up and down the dirt roads of St. John…occasionally glancing at the sky, as my heart pounded with questions about my life. From the looks of my neighborhood, success was graduating high school, getting a state job, and moving in a double-wide trailer somewhere right next to my mom. And maybe that would have been enough, if my heart would have stopped yearning for more.

Have you ever asked God just what are you supposed to be doing on this earth? Have you ever asked God what is your purpose? I call it Life's big question. What is my purpose? The word purpose means a determined end or object to be accomplished. There are so many people that have no idea what God has really called them to accomplish in this earth. Now is the time for us to really seek God's face and get some answers to that question.

Romans 8: 27 - 30 (AMP) says And He Who searches the
hearts of men knows what is in the mind of the
(Holy) Spirit (what His intent is), because the Spirit
intercedes and pleads (before God) in behalf of the
saints according to and in harmony with God's will.
We are assured and know that
(God being a partner in their labor) all things
work together and are [fitting into a plan]
for good to and for those who love God
and are called according to (His) design and purpose.

For those whom He foreknew
(of whom He was aware and loved beforehand),
He also destined from the beginning (foreordaining them)
to be molded into the image of His Son
(and share inwardly His likeness), that He might
become the firstborn among many brethren.
And those whom He thus foreordained,
He also called; and those whom He called,
He also justified (acquitted, made righteous,
putting them into right standing with Himself).
And those whom He justified, He also glorified
(raising them to a heavenly dignity and condition or state of being).

Here's the good news. God has already predestined us for a purpose according to His will. He already has a divine design, a divine mold that He calls a perfect fit for you. So the first step in finding your purpose is to know where to look. And according to Romans 8, looking to God is the only way you will truly find out who He has preordained you to be. Your answer to Life's big question is in God. Just ask Him!

Finding Yourself

So now that you know where to truly find the answer…it's time to get yourself into a position to receive it. I'll admit, along my road to receiving this better life, I made a few pit stops…many times very far away from my true purpose. You know, the life of 40-hour work weeks, twice a month pay…and cubicles instead of offices. It's the life where it seems like your only purpose is to retire and receive a social security check. And when it came to family, true love before finding myself was non-existent. At 26, I was a young mother with two children, a failing marriage and plenty of nay-sayers reminding me that if I got a divorce, no man would ever want me or my children.

So one day, while sitting at my desk at work, I asked God again to please show me my purpose and what I was truly created to do. Sure, I had what the world considered a pretty good job, but my Spirit was searching for much more. It was like a part of me was locked up and I could not find the key. For years, I was in and out of churches searching for directions, searching for the part of my Life that I knew was missing. It seemed like everywhere I went, I could not find anything, and nothing would click. I had perfected hiding my true feelings. On the outside…it looked like all was well…but on the inside I was lonely and depressed. Then, one day, after all the prayers and my searching, everything changed. Someone truly ministered to me about who I was as a woman in the eyes of God. After that, I felt like I had hope again. My Spirit was alive again. From there, I rededicated my life to God, and never looked back.

Today, that same opportunity is available for you. Purpose in your heart that your best life is beginning now.

Revealing God in You

After I rededicated my life, revealing God in me meant removing everything out of my life that was preventing me from fulfilling my destiny. I had to become a single mother again, and I also ended up moving back home with my Mom. From the outside, it seemed as if I was moving backwards, but inside I was following God closer than ever, asking Him at every turn, where do I go from here?

God started by sending me to a ministry, where they helped me cultivate what He was doing on the inside of me. It also helped discipline me in the things of God. The more I sought God, the more He revealed to me the purpose for my Life. I was like Peter in *Matthew 16: 13-20 (AMP)*

Now when Jesus went into the region of Caesarea Philippi, He asked His disciples, Who do people say that the Son of Man is? And they answered, Some say John the Baptist; others say Elijah; and others Jeremiah or one of the prophets. He said to them, But who do you (yourselves) say that I am? Simon Peter replied, You are the Christ, the Son of the Living God. Then Jesus answered him, Blessed (happy, fortunate, and to be envied) are you, Simon Bar-Jonah, for flesh and blood [men] have not revealed this to you, but My Father Who is in heaven. And I tell you, you are Peter (Greek; Petros--a large piece of rock) and on this rock (Greek, petra--a huge rock like Gibraltar) I will build My church, and the gates of Hades (the powers of the infernal region) shall not overpower it (or be strong to its detriment or hold

out against it). I will give you the keys of the kingdom of heaven; and whatever you bind (declare to be improper and unlawful) on earth must be what is already bound in heaven; and whatever you loose (declare lawful) on earth must be what is already loosed in heaven. Then He sternly and strictly charged and warned the disciples to tell no one that He was Jesus the Christ

---

See, because Peter had a revelation from God of who Jesus really was, now Jesus could reveal to Peter who he really was and what his purpose was in Christ. I, like Peter, had to completely surrender my life to God, and truly receive the life he had for me.

1Corinthians 4: 1-2 says so then let us (apostles) be looked upon as ministering servants of Christ and stewards (trustees) of the mysteries (the secret purposes) of God. Moreover, it is (essentially) required of stewards that a man should be found faithful (proving himself worthy of trust).

In other words, we should be trustees over the revealed knowledge our Father has given us, and be found faithful. So what is it that our Father has revealed to you concerning His purpose for your Life? Your purpose has already been pre-ordained, it's already fixed, so all you have to do is unlock the mystery concerning it. And the only way you will fully come to know that purpose, is if the Holy Spirit reveals it to you. Right now, you may feel like you're stuck in a dead-end job, and you may feel frustrated because you are not able to use the gifts and talents that God has given you.

You may also feel like the things in the past are so bad, that there is no longer hope to have a successful life. I declare it is not too late. Now is the time to walk into your God-given destiny.

Hebrews 11:1 says NOW FAITH is the assurance
(the confirmation, the title deed) of the things (we) hope for,
being the proof of things (we) do not see and the
conviction of their reality (faith perceiving as real
fact what is not revealed to the senses).

Working the Mystery

The Word of God is my roadmap to working the mystery that God has placed on the inside of me. The Word of God is a consistent point of reference, and is vital when you have a tremendous calling on your life. In my years of ministering the Word and encouraging people to birth out their destiny, I've experienced a great deal of pain. I know the opportunity to live the God-kind of Life is available for everyone, and I am committed to helping others pursue their destiny. Oftentimes, I have been hurt in wanting something for someone, that they didn't want for themselves. That's why the Word of God has to be your source in determining what's real and what's not. Once you have the Word in hand…it's time to Work It. I can't reiterate how important it is to join a ministry that teaches and encourages you to use your gifts and talents. Make sure it's Holy-Spirit filled and operates as a five-fold ministry. We need the fullness of God in our lives. As men and women on this earth, it is going to take a lot of power and discipline to reach our God-given destiny. It is our discipline that makes us Disciples of Christ. The word disciple actually means disciplined one. Jesus is searching the earth looking for His disciples. Those who are disciplined in their effort to fulfill

God's purpose for their Life.

My second bit of advice for you is to seek God's face like never before. You have to realize the Vision and purpose for your life is really not for you, it's all about the plans and purposes of God. The gifts and talents He has given you are to be planted for increase, so that the Vision of God can be fulfilled in the earth. You have a great calling on your life, and the fulfillment of your destiny is essential to manifesting the Kingdom of God on the earth.

The Kingdom of God

If someone would have told me ten years ago that I would have been living my dreams and fulfilling my purpose at the same time, I would have laughed and kept going, especially considering the pressures that come along with being a spiritual leader. You must understand that when you're pursuing the Kingdom of God, there are many trials and tribulations by Faith. Some people who may start out with you...don't end up with you...because they are only there for a season and a time. It hurts when God tells you to keep moving, and you have to leave others behind. But the Kingdom of God is at hand, and you have to continue to pursue your destiny no matter what!

Matthew 24 talks about the faithful and unfaithful servants. The faithful servant used what God had given and produced more. The unfaithful servant went and hid his talent. Why did the Master call him unfaithful? Because, he didn't use the one talent that God had given him. If he would have planted or used his talent, he would have produced more than the other two servants who had been given the five talents and the two. I know you're asking how could that be, if he had only received one talent? Well, let me show you.

You see, even though the servant had the smallest talent, it would have grown up to be the greatest of all. This is the story of my Life. Come on now, a girl from Quincy, FL…being called to be a prophetess to the nations…Come on!!! But, when I gave my Life to Christ, and began studying on the Kingdom of God and how it really works, my eyes and ears were opened. That's why the scripture says those that have ears to hear, let them hear. Today, I'm walking in my purpose and my destiny. My testimony is that even though the odds were against me, and I was least of all in the world's eyes, I still watered and cultivated the gift God had given me. Now…I'm pushing others to fulfill their destiny. That's what I'm anointed (or endowed with God's power) to do. You have a special anointing too. Maybe it's in the area of business, music, or preaching the gospel.

Whatever comes easy to you, whatever you love to do, your deepest passions and desires, those are the things you need to pray and ask God for a plan, and seek His way of pursuing it. Your peace and prosperity will only be found in the manifestation of your God-given purpose. Once you do what God has called and predestined you to do, you will have nothing missing, lacking, broken, wanted or needed in your Life, and then your salvation will be made whole.

Ecclesiastes 9: 10-11 (AMP)
Whatever your hand finds to do, do it with
all your might, for there is no work or device
or knowledge or wisdom in Sheol (the place of the dead),
where you are going.
I returned and saw under the sun that
the race is not to the swift nor the battle to
the strong, neither is bread to the wise
nor riches to men of intelligence and
understanding nor favor to men of skill;
but time and chance happen to them all.

We must rise to the occasion! We must realize Now Is Our Time, Now Is Our Chance, and We Are Approved To Do It. God has already justified us (Romans 8:30-33). God has already given us His stamp of approval. It's already done, so pursue your passion, pursue your dream, grab hold and stand firm in your God-given destiny.

Romans 8:37-39 (KJV)
Nay, in all these things we are more than conquerors
through him that loved us. For I am persuaded,
that neither death, nor life, nor angels, nor principalities,
nor powers, nor things present, nor things to come, nor height,
nor depth, nor any other creature, shall be able to separate
us from the love of God, which is in Christ Jesus our Lord.

II.
Plan

For I know the thoughts and plans that I have for you, says the Lord, thoughts and plans for welfare and peace and not for evil, to give you hope in your final outcome.
Jeremiah 29:11 AMP

Mapping It All Out

The Kingdom of God system is all about doing things God's way to produce the God-kind of results. I had to develop a new plan for my Life, one where God was the head and I was open to follow. Before I knew my purpose, I had not considered helping to Pastor a church, but God knew the plans He had for me. First things first, you must pray and fast for God's plans to be revealed to you.

If you're in a horrible situation right now, you must stand assured that God has a better plan for your Life. You have to make a Godly road map for your Life. There may be a lot of bumps and roadblocks in your way such as sin, poverty, lack, sickness, disease, divorce, or any past mistakes. Maybe you had children outside of the covenant of marriage. I'm here to tell you…whatever it is…***Don't let your past mistakes be the foundation for your future.*** God is doing a new thing in you.

Isaiah 43:18-19
Remember ye not the former things,
neither consider the things of old.
Behold, I will do a new thing; now it shall
spring forth; shall ye not know it?
I will even make a way in the wilderness,
and rivers in the desert.

God will restore back to us everything that has been taken from us.

---

*Joel 2:25 -28 (AMP) says And I will restore
or replace for you the years that the locust has
eaten--the hopping locust, the stripping locust,
and the crawling locust, My great army which I sent
among you. And you shall eat in plenty and be
satisfied and praise the name of the Lord,
your God, Who has dealt wondrously with you.
And My people shall never be put to shame.
And you shall know, understand, and realize
that I am in the midst of Israel and that I
the Lord am your God and there is none else.
My people shall never be put to shame.
And afterward I will pour out My Spirit
upon all flesh; and your sons and your
daughters shall prophesy, your old men
shall dream dreams, your young men shall see visions.*

Once God restores you, then it's time to write the Vision for your life.

---

*Habakkuk 2:2-3 (AMP) says
And the Lord answered me and said,
Write the vision and engrave it so plainly
upon tablets that everyone who passes
may (be able to) read (it easily and quickly)
as he hastens by. For the vision is yet for
an appointed time and it hastens to the end
(fulfillment); it will not deceive or disappoint.
Though it tarry, wait (earnestly) for it,
because it will surely come; it will not be
behindhand on its appointed day.*

When I truly got a revelation of what it meant to trust and truly depend on the Word of God to help write the Vision for my life, I realized I had entered the realm of fail-proof living. I was truly walking by Faith, and even though at times, circumstances and people would try to make me feel like I was doing something wrong, I finally had a revelation that the Word of God was my foundation. It was my foundation of faith. So I want to encourage you, when the opposition comes to wreak havoc on your plans, remember your foundation. God cannot fail, and He cannot lie. So therefore, if He has it planned for you, as long as you continue to show up...it will surely come to pass. I've witnessed it firsthand in my Life. Every time I showed up, God showed Himself strong through me. Time and time again God has shown me that what He has purposed for me is far greater than any man can see.

Jeremiah 29: 11 says For I know the thoughts
and plans that I have for you, says the Lord,
thoughts and plans for welfare and peace
and not for evil, to give you hope in your final outcome.

It sounds to me that God has plans to prosper you. He has plans to give you everything you ever wanted or needed to produce the God-kind of Life. The word produce means to present or bring into view, to show something out for people to see or partake, and to bear. Here's a warning though. If a farmer doesn't produce in his season, then he doesn't make a profit, and thus he doesn't prosper. God has placed some pretty big seeds on the inside of each and every one of us, and now He's calling for us to prosper in the Kingdom of God.

Psalms 92:12-15 (KJV) says The righteous shall flourish like the palm tree: he shall grow like a cedar in Lebanon. Those that be planted in the house of the LORD shall flourish in the courts of our God. They shall still bring forth fruit in old age; they shall be fat and flourishing; To shew that the LORD is upright: He is my rock, and there is no unrighteousness in Him.

You see…God wants to bring forth His plans for your Life, so He can show the nations that He is upright. God is using me, my family, and my ministry as a testimony for you to see that the Lord is upright. It was the Lord who established me, called me, and ordained me…even from the foundation of this world. And guess what…He has done the same for you! It's time now to walk in it…and refuse to let anyone or anything take you off your path to destiny.

Stay On The Road

> *Hebrews 11:1 says NOW FAITH is the assurance*
> *(the confirmation, the title deed) of the things (we) hope for, being*
> *the proof of things (we) do not see and the conviction of their reality*
> *(faith perceiving as real fact what is not revealed to the senses).*

Now Faith, for me, meant making a quality decision to change my life, and not take no for an answer. The moment you decide to Live the life God has purposed for you…Now Faith will allow you to begin writing the plan to pursue your destiny. When I walked away from my old life years ago…I never turned back! This book is the first book I ever authored, and is a product of the small steps I take each day by Faith. The key now is to continue in "Now Faith," and believe that with every step we are inching closer and closer towards the fullness of our destiny. Just remember, what you're doing right now is the foundation of the things that you are hoping for and the evidence and proof that you already have them. Selah (Think about that). Now Is The Time for the things of God to be made manifest in your Life.

III.
Pursuit

For He says, In the time of favor
(of an assured welcome) I have listened
to and heeded your call, and I have
helped you on the day of deliverance
(the day of salvation). Behold, now is
truly the time for a gracious welcome and
acceptance (of you from God); behold,
now is the day of salvation!
2Corinthians 6:2 AMP

Now Is My Time

Once God revealed His purpose for my life and helped me compile a new plan, the foundation was set and ready for me to pursue my destiny. It's at this point that you come to realize just how serious God is about Kingdom business. He has designed you for something, and now...He's taken away every excuse you have not do it. There were plenty of times when I felt like it was too much for me to handle, but God reminded me that it was Him...not me, who was working within me to fulfill my destiny. All I had to do was show-up and pursue it. Pursue means to go after something with the intent to overtake or accomplish. Whatever the Vision or Purpose is for our Lives, we have to go after it until it is accomplished. It's all about production in the Kingdom of God. He wants to see some fruit from the things He has planted within us. This is the time of reckoning. The Lord is coming to see what you've done with the gifts and talents He's given you.

So from reading this scripture, it shows us how important it is to produce the fruit on the inside of us. We don't want to be among those taking up room, depleting the soil. We have to live productive lives and produce the Word of God.

We have to be producers of God's Word in this earth. I often envision the Kingdom of God being like a Movie. Our Lord Jesus is the Executive Producer and Writer, and we are the ones who take the script and produce what Jesus has put in place for us. Now Is Our Time To Produce!

The Challenge

There will come a time along your Faith-walk when excuses will become irrelevant, and God will say to you, "I'm not asking you…I'm telling you!" You must realize you are just one of many players in God's grand purpose of spreading salvation throughout the earth. I want to challenge you to pursue your purpose in the Kingdom.

Genesis 8:22 (AMP) says while the earth remains, seedtime and harvest, cold and heat, summer and winter, and day and night shall not cease.

So with that said, you still have time to harvest the seed that God has planted inside of you. The fact that you are reading this book right now is evidence that God is still in the producing business. Right now you're reading the manifestation of a seed God placed in me long before I even knew I had a purpose in Christ to fulfill.

*Luke 8:11-15 (AMP) says now the meaning of
the parable is this: The seed is the Word of God.
Those along the traveled road are the people who have heard;
then the devil comes and carries away the message
out of their hearts, that they may not believe
(acknowledge Me as their Savior and devote themselves to Me)
and be saved (here and hereafter).
And those upon the rock (are the people) who,
when they hear (the Word), receive and welcome
it with joy; but these have no root. They believe for a while,
and in time of trial and temptation fall away
(withdraw and stand aloof). And as for what
fell among the thorns, these are [the people]
who hear, but as they go on their way they are
choked and suffocated with the anxieties and
cares and riches and pleasures of life, and their
fruit does not ripen (come to maturity and perfection).
But as for that (seed) in the good soil, these are
(the people) who, hearing the Word, hold it
fast in a just, noble, virtuous) and worthy heart,
and steadily bring forth fruit with patience.*

Make up your mind right now, and stand committed to receive the Word of God on good ground. Simply put, the type of ground you are will determine the Harvest. It's time to overcome ourselves. God said if He spoke it, He shall bring it to pass. His Word will do exactly what He purposed it to do. That means the things that you think are holding you back from pursuing your destiny, have already been overthrown by the power of God.

Matthew 16:18-19 says (AMP) And I tell you,
you are (Peter)Greek, Petros--a large piece of rock],
and on this rock (Greek, petra--a huge rock like Gibraltar)
I will build My church, and the gates of Hades
(the powers of the infernal region) shall not
overpower it (or be strong to its detriment
or hold out against it). I will give you the keys
of the kingdom of heaven; and whatever
you bind (declare to be improper and unlawful)
on earth must be what is already bound in heaven;
and whatever you loose (declare lawful) on earth
must be what is already loosed in heaven.

You have to be confident and know that you already have the victory over every evil work, over every circumstance, every sickness and disease, and every foul spirit. You also have the authority and the power to trample over serpents and scorpions. God has given you physical and mental strength and ability over all the power that the enemy possesses, and nothing shall in any way harm you. Nothing shall stop you from pursuing your destiny in Christ. **You Have The Power.**

Isaiah 54:16 -17 (AMP) says; Behold, I have created
the smith who blows on the fire of coals and
who produces a weapon for its purpose; and I have created
the devastator to destroy. But no weapon that is formed
against you shall prosper, and every tongue that shall rise
against you in judgment you shall show to be in the wrong. This
(peace, righteousness, security, triumph over opposition) is
the heritage of the servants of the Lord [those in whom the ideal
Servant of the Lord is reproduced]; this is the righteousness or the
vindication which they obtain from Me (this is that which
I impart to them as their justification), says the Lord.

God says that He created the smith (the thing that is harassing you). God created everything, and we're His servants. So why aren't we pursuing the inheritance that God has laid up for us? We must pursue it. We are the true servants of the Lord.

As servants, we have Salvation (Soteria), which means we have the fullness of peace (nothing missing, lacking, broken, wanted, or needed), protection, welfare, and prosperity (wholeness) in our Lives. So what is it that is holding you back from pursuing your God-given destiny?

There have been so many things that could have kept me from getting to this point in my Life. From poverty/lack and low self-esteem, to looking for love in all the wrong places. Or how about the fact that I didn't go to college or the generational curses that were on my family. Still, through all the circumstances, I made it to where I am today. Now, I live my Life everyday pursuing the purposes and plans of God for me. And the best part is, my children and their children can now be partakers in the God-kind of life, and live to pursue their purpose as well. It's your turn now, don't delay, for the Kingdom of Heaven is truly at hand. Remember, **Don't Let Your Past Mistakes Be The Foundation Of Your Future. Now Is Your Time!**

About Nicky Yarborough

NOW FAITH is the assurance (the confirmation, the title deed) of the things (we) hope for, being the proof of things (we) do not see and the conviction of their reality (faith perceiving as real fact what is not revealed to the senses). Hebrews 11:1 AMP

Nicky Yarborough

It's refreshing, it's pure, and it's packed with a Word to push you into your destiny. The ministry gift of Nicky Yarborough is inspiring people to fulfill their God-given purpose by breaking free from Life's bondages and seeing the end of their Faith. Born July 12, 1974 in Quincy, FL, Nicky Yarborough's faith- filled teachings are packed with revelation knowledge that far exceeds her age.

Nicky received the gift of salvation at the age of 12, at St. John Church of God in Christ under the leadership of the Late Bishop E.L. Shepphard. Nearly 15 years later she rededicated her life to Christ and began serving at Neighborhood Outreach Christian Center in Quincy, FL. She became a licensed and ordained minister on August 17, 2003, and began spreading the gospel through the vehicle of Nicky Yarborough Ministries.

Since 2003, Nicky's reach has increased, and today she's taken her ministry gift online...establishing a new web ministry... NowIsMyTime.org. The site serves as a global point of reference for people who are set on pursuing their destiny. Additionally, Nicky's outreach efforts have increased and includes prison ministry, teen mentoring seminars, community clothing drives, and various conferences and seminars. Now a published author, her book, "Discovering You," is a testimony of how she overcame an ordinary life to pursue an extraordinary life in Christ.

Nicky's overall Vision is to teach the nations how to use the Word of God to build a foundation of Faith. From her very first women's conference, "No More Chains" back in 2004, to her new ministry... "Life In The Now," she is set on taking her message of "Now Faith" *(Hebrews 11:1)* around the world.

As a Minister, Speaker, Author, and Mother, Nicky says the key to balancing it all is having the right foundation. Hebrews 11:1...Now Faith.

To request Nicky Yarborough for an upcoming event...visit us online at www.nowismytime.org

Daily Confessions

I am The Body of Christ and Satan has no power over me. *1Corinthians 12:2*

I am of God and overcome Satan. For greater is He that is in me, than he that is in the world. *1John 4:4*

I will fear no evil, for Thou art with me, Lord, Your Word and Your Spirit they comfort me. *Psalms 23:4*

I am far from oppression, and fear does not come nigh me. *Isaiah 54:14*

There is no lack, for my God supplies all my needs according to His riches in glory in Christ Jesus. *Philippians 4:19*

The Lord has pleasure in the prosperity of His servants, and Abraham's blessings are mine. *Psalms 35:27; Galatians 3:14*

I trust in the Lord with all my heart, and lean not unto my own understanding. *John 16:13*

The Lord will perfect that which concerns me. *Psalms 138:8*

I am filled with the knowledge of the Lord's will in all wisdom and spiritual understanding. *Colossians 1:19*

I have put off the old man and have put on the new man, which is renewed in the knowledge of Him; *Ephesians 1:17*

I am born of God and I have world-overcoming faith residing on the inside of me. *John 5:4*

I will do all things through Christ which strengthens me. *Philippians 4:13*

The joy of the Lord is my strength. The Lord is the strength of my life. *Nehemiah 8:10*

I let no corrupt communication proceed out of my mouth, but that which is good for edifying, that it may minister grace to the hearer. *Ephesians 4:29*

I delight myself in the Lord and He gives me the desires of my heart. *Psalms 37:4*

I am an overcomer and I overcome by the blood of the Lamb and the word of my testimony. *Revelation 12:11*

The Word of God is forever settled in heaven. Therefore, I established His Word upon this Earth. *Psalms 119:89*

Heal me, O Lord, and I shall be healed; save Me, and I shall be saved: for thou art my praise. *Jeremiah 17:14*

The Lord is my Rock, and my Fortress, and my Deliverer; My God, my Strength, in whom I will trust; My Buckler, and the horn of My Salvation, and My High Tower. *Psalms 18:2*

Nay, in all these things I am more than a conqueror through Him that loved Me. *Romans 8:37*

If I abide in the Lord, and His Word abides in me, I shall ask whatever I want, and it shall be done unto me. *John 15:7*

Discovering You

If you enjoyed this book, we'd love to hear from you! E-mail us at discoveringyou@nowismytime.org

Additional Books
The Promise Devotional...31-Days of God's Promises For Your Life